HAL•LEONARD INSTRUMENTAL PLAY-ALONG

CELLO

AUDIO ACCESS INCLUDED

PLAYBACK+
Speed • Pitch • Balance • Loop

Disney
BEAUTY AND THE

To access audio visit:
www.halleonard.com/mylibrary

Enter Code
3084-6355-0716-8653

ISBN 978-1-4950-9619-8

Motion Picture Artwork, TM & Copyright
© 2017 Disney Enterprises, Inc.

**Wonderland Music Company, Inc.
Walt Disney Music Company**

DISTRIBUTED BY

HAL•LEONARD®

7777 W. BLUEMOUND RD. P.O. BOX 13819 MILWAUKEE, WI 53213

In Australia Contact:
Hal Leonard Australia Pty. Ltd.
4 Lentara Court
Cheltenham, Victoria, 3192 Australia
Email: ausadmin@halleonard.com.au

Visit Hal Leonard Online at
www.halleonard.com

ARIA

CELLO

Music by ALAN MENKEN
Lyrics by TIM RICE

BE OUR GUEST

CELLO

Music by ALAN MENKEN
Lyrics by HOWARD ASHMAN

BEAUTY AND THE BEAST

Music by ALAN MENKEN
Lyrics by HOWARD ASHMAN

CELLO

BELLE

CELLO

Music by ALAN MENKEN
Lyrics by HOWARD ASHMAN

8

DAYS IN THE SUN

CELLO

Music by ALAN MENKEN
Lyrics by TIM RICE

EVERMORE

CELLO

Music by ALAN MENKEN
Lyrics by TIM RICE

GASTON

CELLO

Music by ALAN MENKEN
Lyrics by HOWARD ASHMAN

HOW DOES A MOMENT LAST FOREVER

CELLO

Music by ALAN MENKEN
Lyrics by TIM RICE

THE MOB SONG

CELLO

Music by ALAN MENKEN
Lyrics by HOWARD ASHMAN

SOMETHING THERE

CELLO

Music by ALAN MENKEN
Lyrics by HOWARD ASHMAN